Contents

Any words appearing in the text in bold, **like this**, are explained in the glossary.

Looking at buildings

People plan and construct buildings for many reasons. People live, worship, go to events, and work in buildings. Buildings are places where people come together. How they look can often give us a clue about what they are used for.

Religion

This building is used by people who follow the religion of Buddhism. This religion started in India in the 6th century BCE. Most Japanese towns and cities have Buddhist temples, which often include a main hall, like this one, a gateway, and a cemetery where people are buried.

Todai Temple, Nara, Japan, 745–753 CE

This temple is one of the world's largest wooden structures.

WHAT IS ART?

Buildings

KAREN HOSACK

www.raintreepublishers.co.uk
Visit our website to find out more information about Raintree books.

To order:
☎ Phone 44 (0) 1865 888112
▤ Send a fax to 44 (0) 1865 314091
▢ Visit the Raintree Bookshop at www.raintreepublishers.co.uk to browse our catalogue and order online

Raintree is an imprint of Capstone Global Library Limited, a company incorporated in England and Wales having its registered office at 7 Pilgrim Street, London, EC4V 6LB – Registered company number: 6695582

"Raintree" is a registered trademark of Pearson Education Limited, under licence to Capstone Global Library Limited

Editorial: Adam Miller, Charlotte Guillain, Clare Lewis and Catherine Veitch
Design: Victoria Bevan and AMR Design Ltd
Illustrations: David Woodroffe
Picture Research: Mica Brancic
Production: Victoria Fitzgerald

Originated by Dot Gradations Ltd, UK
Printed and bound by CTPS (China Translation & Printing Services Ltd)

ISBN 978 1 4062 0942 6 (hardback)
12 11 10 09 08
10 9 8 7 6 5 4 3 2 1

ISBN 978 1 4062 0949 5 (paperback)
13 12 11 10 09
10 9 8 7 6 5 4 3 2 1

British Library Cataloguing in Publication Data Hosack, Karen
    Buildings. - (What is art?)
    1. Architecture - Juvenile literature 2. Architecture - Appreciation - Juvenile literature
    I. Title
    720
A full catalogue record for this book is available from the British Library.

Acknowledgements

The publishers would like to thank the following for permission to reproduce photographs:
©Alamy pp. **5** (Ian Dagnall), **11** (Travelshots.com), **19** (PCL), **22** (Images Etc Ltd), **24** (Peter Barritt); ©Corbis pp. **4** (Christophe Boisvieux), **7** (Richard Cooke), **8** (Arcaid), **18** (Danny Lehman), **26** (Rudy Sulgan); ©Dreamstime p. **21**; ©Getty pp. **9** (Axiom Photographic Agency), **13** (Romilly Lockyer), **15** (Tim Boyle), **27** (Stone+/Stephen Schauer); ©istockphoto pp. **6** (fotoVoyager), **10** (David Iliff), **14** (H Peter Weber), **20** (Lawrence Freytag), **23** (Klaas Lingbeek-van Kranen); ©Rex Features pp. **12** (Andrew Drysdale), **16** (Eye Ubiquitous), **17** (Stock Connection/Cosmo Condina); ©2008 Banco de México Diego Rivera & Frieda Kahlo Museums Trust. Av. Cinco de Mayo No.2, Col. Centro, Del. Cuauhtémoc 06059, México, D.F0 Scala Art Library p. **25**.

Cover photograph of Atrium of Santiago Grand Hyatt Hotel, Santiago, Chile reproduced with permission of Corbis/ Richard T. Nowitz.

Every effort has been made to contact copyright holders of any material reproduced in this book.
Any omissions will be rectified in subsequent printings if notice is given to the publishers.

Disclaimer

All the Internet addresses (URLs) given in this book were valid at time of going to press. However, due to the dynamic nature of the Internet, some addresses may have changed, or sites may have changed or ceased to exist since publication. While the author and publishers regret any inconvenience this may cause readers, no responsibility for any such changes can be accepted by either the author or the publishers. It is recommended that adults supervise children on the Internet.

As a place for showing exhibitions, why do you think this building needs large spaces?

Did you know?

Architecture is the word we give to different styles and types of buildings. Architects are people who design buildings.

Pompidou Centre, Paris, France, 1972–76

Art

The Pompidou Centre in Paris, France, is an amazing building with many large glass windows so we can see almost all the way through it. It was **designed** as a museum and art gallery. One problem the **architect** had was where to hide the pipes for the air conditioning and water supply. He solved the problem by making them part of the building's design and painting the pipes in bright colours.

5

Homes

Architects designed both of these buildings as homes. What do they say about the people who live in them?

Palaces and castles

Buckingham Palace is the official home of the Queen of England and her family. It has been the London home of British kings and queens since 1837. The royal family uses many of its 600 rooms for special events, such as banquets for leaders of other countries. There are many famous works of art and antique furniture in these rooms, and some are open to the public as a museum.

Buckingham Palace, London, 1705

Would you like having your home opened up to the public?

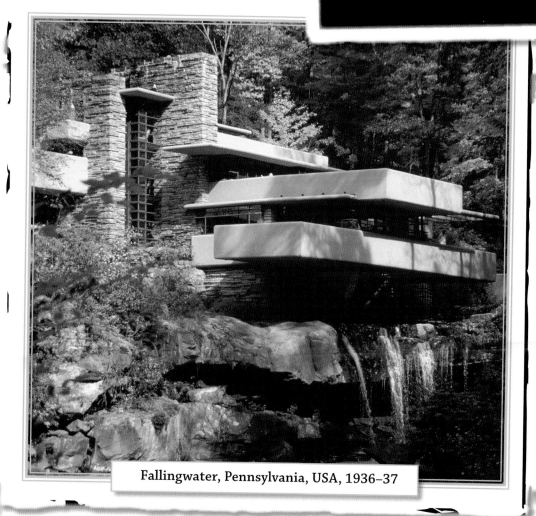

Fallingwater, Pennsylvania, USA, 1936–37

Natural surroundings

The American architect Frank Lloyd Wright believed that the buildings he **designed** should fit in with nature. He thought this would affect the way people lived their lives. This is one of the architect's most famous designs for a private home. You can see how it is surrounded by trees and the waterfall seems to come from the building.

Think about it!
Think about your own home. What makes it different from public buildings, such as schools, libraries, or shops?

Ideas from nature

The **architects** who **designed** these two buildings also got ideas from the natural world.

Trees or bones?

The Spanish architect Antoni Gaudí designed very unusual buildings. Many of them are in Barcelona. They seem to grow from the ground with their curved edges and tree-like structures, although most are made from **concrete**. There are very few straight lines and one side of a building does not always match the other. We call this **organic** architecture.

Casa Batllo, Barcelona, Spain, 1904–1906

People in Barcelona call this building the 'House of Bones' because they think the columns look like bones. Other people think they look like elephants' legs.

Bird or fish?

The Milwaukee Art Museum is on the banks of Lake Michigan. The building includes a giant sunscreen that opens out like wings when the museum is open. It looks a bit like a giant bird sitting at the side of the lake. The wings even flap each day at noon to entertain visitors to the museum.

Did you know?

The Austrian architect Friedensreich Hundertwasser built colourful and unusually shaped buildings in Vienna. He included trees and plants on balconies and the roof so that nature was a key part of his buildings.

Milwaukee Art Museum, Wisconsin, USA, 1994–2001

Do you think the building looks like a bird, or a huge fish?

Large public spaces

The Colosseum is a large Roman building that was finished in 82 CE. It is called an **amphitheatre** and up to 50,000 people could sit inside. It was used for large public events such as gladiator fights, executions, and plays. Its round shape with the stage in the centre meant that everyone had a good view of the action.

Did you know?
Today the Colosseum is partly ruined because of earthquakes and people taking the stones. But it is still a very popular tourist attraction and a reminder of Rome's ancient history.

Many people would gather in the Colosseum to be entertained.

The Colosseum, Rome, Italy, 70–82 CE

This theatre, called the Globe, was designed in a similar way to the Colosseum. The audience are closer to the drama because the stage is in the centre of the building. The first Globe was built from wood and **thatch** in London in 1599, and many of Shakespeare's plays were performed there. In 1613 it accidentally burnt down. A second building was built in the same place before Shakespeare died but it was closed and knocked down in 1644.

The Globe, London, 1997

This photograph shows the new Globe theatre, which was built near the site of the old Globe. It was opened in 1997.

Celebrating an age

Some buildings are **designed** to celebrate their time in history. The **Industrial Revolution** was a time of great change in the world. One of these changes was the invention of the steam railway. People were looking to the future with hope and excitement. A station building was therefore a very good way to show this feeling of celebration. Paddington station in London has a beautiful arched roof made of glass and wrought iron. We get an idea of the wealth at the time from this heavily decorated roof and the stone figures around the front entrance.

Paddington station was designed by Isambard Kingdom Brunel who also designed many other buildings, bridges, and tunnels in the 19th century.

Paddington Station, London, 1852–1854

Biggest and best?

In the 1920s there was competition between **architects** to produce the tallest building in the world. The Eiffel Tower in Paris was the tallest structure for some time but the Chrysler Building in New York overtook it in 1930. The building was the dream of the car manufacturer Walter P. Chrysler. It did not keep the title of tallest building for long. One year after it was finished, the Empire State Building was built.

At the top of the Chrysler Building there are **gargoyles** in the shape of car ornaments.

Chrysler Building, New York, USA, 1926–30

Materials

The Chrysler Building was mainly made from metal. Today, people are starting to use more natural materials that are better for the environment. In Scandinavia, people have been living in wooden buildings for a long time. The wood is specially treated so that moisture cannot damage the house. The trees come from **sustainable** forests and less energy is used to produce green buildings.

Log home, Scandinavia

Wooden houses that are made of trees from sustainable forests are known as 'green buildings'.

Green roofs

For centuries people have used natural materials to **insulate** their homes. **Thatched** roofs were very popular, but fire could easily damage them. Today, some people use the natural warmth of soil and grass on the roof to protect a building. It is important that the roof is waterproof and that water can drain away well.

Did you know?

Today, people are using more and more natural materials to build. Some people are building their houses out of straw bales. This is a cheaper way of building that is good for the environment. The bales also insulate the house very well.

Rooftop garden on City Hall, Chicago, USA, 2001

In large cities today there is little space for gardens or parks. Some people like to turn their roofs into green spaces.

Old and new

This strange looking building is known as the 'Gherkin'.
Can you see why? This modern building is close to the historic
centre of London, where there are many old and famous buildings.
It was designed to be as good for the environment as possible.
The huge glass windows bring a large amount of daylight into
the building, so people do not need to turn on lights. Air is brought
into the building in natural ways so that the people who work
there do not always use air-conditioning.

Swiss Re Tower (the 'Gherkin'), London, 2001–2004

How do you think
people reacted to
the 'Gherkin' when
it was being built?

Think about it!

Some people believe that any new buildings constructed next to old buildings should match in style and materials. Other people think it is more interesting to show something new and different. What do you think?

The Louvre Pyramid, Paris, France, 1989

Does it fit?

The Louvre is a very famous art museum in Paris. In 1989, a modern glass pyramid was added to the much-loved building. Many people could not understand how a structure so different in shape and materials could sit alongside the much older museum. However, over time people have started to like the new building and think it celebrates their own age.

Cities and their buildings

Large cities are often built around rivers or on the coast. This is because water used to be the fastest way of moving materials and people.

Venice

The city of Venice is spread over a number of islands that are joined together by canals. Many of the beautiful buildings that survive today were built in the time of the **Renaissance**, when many artists and designers lived in Venice. Light reflects off the water in the canals onto the light stone and marble architecture.

Today, pollution and damage to the foundations of the city are big problems in Venice.

Chicago's Skyline

The Chicago skyline is one of the world's most impressive. Three out of America's five tallest buildings are located here. Construction is underway on the Chicago Spire, which will be the tallest building in America and the second tallest in the world!

The Chicago **skyline** is much more modern than Venice. It also grew up next to water, in this case Lake Michigan. The lake is now reflected in many of the numerous skyscrapers that show the city's success and wealth.

Places of power

The Capitol, in Washington, D.C., USA, looks very impressive with its large dome. Work began on it in 1793. The Capitol has two large wings on either side of the dome. One is for the House of Representatives, the other is for the Senate. These two groups make up **Congress**. Congress is responsible for making the laws in the United States.

The Capitol, Washington, D.C., USA, 1793

President George Washington laid the **cornerstone** of the Capitol.

The large clock tower on the side of the building is known as Big Ben. It is named after the bell inside the tower.

The Houses of Parliament, London, 1870

The Houses of Parliament in London are famous all over the world. Governments have ruled from this place for over a thousand years. This building was finished in 1870. It is home to the British government and serves the same purpose as the Capitol Building in the United States.

Symbolic building

The White House is the official home of the President of the United States of America. When we see an image of the White House on television we know that the report is about the US government and not about the building itself.

Memorials

Some buildings are made to remember a person. They remind us about an individual's achievements or how much they were loved by those left behind.

The Taj Mahal in India was built by Emperor Shah Jahan in memory of his wife. The massive white marble building was constructed between 1632 and 1647. The craftsmanship is amazing, especially as it was done without the help of modern technology. The beautiful balance of the building is reflected in the water at the front, making it look as though it is floating.

Taj Mahal, Agra, India, 1632–47

How do you think the Emperor felt about his wife?

Do you think Lincoln would have been pleased with his memorial?

Lincoln Memorial, Washington, D.C., USA, 1914–22

Public memory

This memorial was built in memory of the 16th president of the United States of America, Abraham Lincoln. The building is made up of 36 columns, one column for each American state at the time. Inside, there is a 6-metre (19-foot) high sculpture of Lincoln sitting and thinking. The site of the memorial is now used for many large public gatherings and **political** protests.

On the inside

The inside of a building can be as interesting as the outside. Buildings can come to life when there is decoration on the walls, floors, and ceilings.

This Italian **Renaissance** ceiling painting was started in 1508 and finished in 1512. It is painted on plaster using a technique called **fresco**. The plaster had to be damp so that it didn't absorb the oil paint too much. This meant the artist and his assistants needed to work very quickly. Once you know this, the painting becomes even more impressive.

The Sistine Chapel, Rome, Italy, 1512

You can see this ceiling in the Sistine Chapel in Rome, Italy. It is part of the official residence of the Pope, the Roman Catholic leader.

Frescoes

Frescoes can be seen in many religious buildings and people's homes from this time. They are very fragile and can be damaged by damp conditions.

What does this mural tell us about how people spent their leisure time? What clothes did they wear to go to the park?

Dream of a Sunday Afternoon in the Alameda Park by Diego Rivera, 1947–48

During the Great Depression in the 1930s, people in the United States began painting frescoes. Artists were given money to set up projects by the Works Progress Administration (known as WPA). Many thousands of workers took part to show what ordinary American people were feeling and the frescoes were put in places where many people would gather. These **murals** tell us about what was important to people at the time.

Buildings all around us

In this book we have looked at many reasons why people **design** and construct buildings. We have also looked at different materials that **architects** use and how buildings can represent a variety of things.

Buildings are part of our everyday life. It is very easy to just walk past them without thinking too much about why they are there and who might have designed them.

The Empire State Building is the tallest building in New York. It is a very well known symbol of the city.

Empire State Building, New York, USA, 1931

Look again at your home and at the buildings where you live. Can you see anything that you have never noticed before?

Clapboard home, California, USA

Buildings become very familiar to us and can actually make us feel 'at home'. You might think about a landmark near to where you live as being 'home'. You probably think that the building you live in with your family is the place you belong. We really can become attached to the buildings around us.

Timeline

Where to see buildings

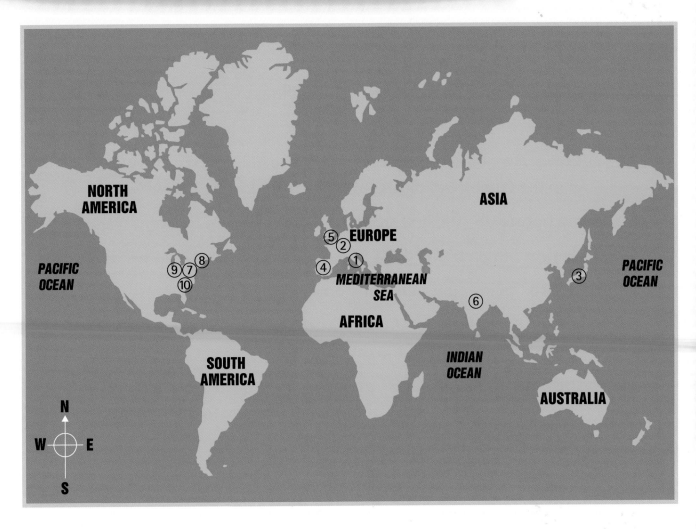

This map shows where you can see some of the buildings in this book.

(1) Rome, Italy
    The Sistine Chapel
    The Colosseum
(2) Paris, France
    Pompidou Centre
    The Louvre Pyramid
(3) Nara, Japan
    Todai Temple
(4) Barcelona, Spain
    Casa Batllo

(5) London, UK
    The Houses of
        Parliament
    Shakespeare's Globe
    Buckingham Palace
    Paddington Station
    Swiss Re Tower
(6) India
    Taj Mahal

(7) Washington, D.C., USA:
    The White House
    Lincoln Memorial
(8) New York City, USA
    Chrysler Building
    Empire State Building
(9) Chicago, USA
    City Hall
(10) Pennsylvania, USA
    Fallingwater

Glossary

amphitheatre circular building with no roof and with rows of seating

architect person who designs buildings

concrete mixture of sand, cement and water used in building

Congress both the Senate and House of Representatives meet in the Capitol building and make laws for the United States

cornerstone the first stone laid down when a building is built

design to plan and draw pictures of how something will look

fresco painting that is done on damp plaster

gargoyle a face or figure in the roof of a building, sometimes forming a spout from a gutter

Industrial Revolution period of time in the 19th century when more machinery and factories began to be used

insulate to use some sort of material to keep heat inside a building or other object

mural picture painted straight onto a wall

organic how plants and animals grow naturally

political interest in how countries are governed

Renaissance period of European history between the fourteenth and sixteenth centuries when there was a renewed interest in art

skyline outline of hills and buildings

sustainable to ensure a future

thatch roofing made of straw or reeds

Learn more

Books to read

Buildings at Work: Syscrapers, Elisabeth Encarnacio and Hannah Ray (QED Publishing, 2008)

Building Amazing Structures: Skyscrapers, Chris Oxlade (Heinemann Library, 2006)

Building Amazing Structures: Stadiums, Chris Oxlade (Heinemann Library, 2006)

Eco Action: Buildings of the Future, Angela Royston (Heinemann Library, 2007)

Websites to visit

Visit the kid's section of the official Empire State Building website.

www.esbnyc.com/kids/index

Explore the Taj Mahal and learn all about its past.

www.tajmahal.org.uk

Discover the work of many great architects.

www.greatbuildings.com/architects

Index